Congratulations!

Follow Quote Octopus on Social Media for FREE Books And the Chance to Win Incredible Daily Prizes!

Facebook.com/QuoteOctopus

Twitter.com/QuoteOctopus

Youtube.com/QuoteOctopus

Today you are you! That is truer than true! There is no one alive who is you-er than you!

Dr. Seuss

A birthday is just another day where you go to work and people give you love. Age is just a state of mind, and you are as old as you think you are. You have to count your blessings and be happy.

Abhishek Bachchan

There are two great days in a person's life - the day we are born and the day we discover why.

William Barclay

The more you praise and celebrate your life, the more there is in life to celebrate.

Oprah Winfrey

Cakes are special. Every birthday, every celebration ends with something sweet, a cake, and people remember. It's all about the memories.

Buddy Valastro

Age is a case of mind over matter. If you don't mind, it don't matter.

Satchel Paige

The greatest gift that you can give to others is the gift of unconditional love and acceptance.

Brian Tracy

How old would you be if you didn't know how old you are?

Satchel Paige

Don't just count your years, make your years count.

George Meredith

If you look over the years, the styles have changed - the clothes, the hair, the production, the approach to the songs. The icing to the cake has changed flavors. But if you really look at the cake itself, it's really the same.

John Oates

You don't get older, you get better.

Shirley Bassey

The greatest gifts you can give your children are the roots of responsibility and the wings of independence.

Denis Waitley

Every year on your birthday, you get a chance to start new.

Sammy Hagar

You take away all the other luxuries in life, and if you can make someone smile and laugh, you have given the most special gift: happiness.

Brad Garrett

I don't pay attention to the number of birthdays. It's weird when I say I'm 53. It just is crazy that I'm 53. I think I'm very immature. I feel like a kid. That's why my back goes out all the time, because I completely forget I can't do certain things anymore - like doing the plank for 10 minutes.

Ellen DeGeneres

The way I see it, you should live everyday like its your birthday.

Paris Hilton

You know you're getting old when the candles cost more than the cake.

Bob Hope

The great thing about getting older is that you don't lose all the other ages you've been.

Madeleine L'Engle

We have to be able to grow up. Our wrinkles are our medals of the passage of life. They are what we have been through and who we want to be.

Lauren Hutton

All the world is birthday cake, so take a piece, but not too much.

George Harrison

Presents don't really mean much to me. I don't want to sound mawkish, but - it was the realization that I have a great many people in my life who really love me, and who I really love.

Gabriel Byrne

For my birthday this year, my girlfriends - who knew I'd just inherited my dad's turntable - gave me a carton of albums like 'Blue Kentucky Girl,' by Emmylou Harris, and 'Off the Wall,' by Michael Jackson. It's all stuff we grew up with. I mean, you can't have a music collection without Prince's 'Purple Rain' - it just can't be done!

Connie Britton

It takes a long time to become young.

Pablo Picasso

I like birthday cake. It's so symbolic. It's a tempting symbol to load with something more complicated than just 'Happy birthday!' because it's this emblem of childhood and a happy day.

Aimee Bender

The only thing better than singing is more singing.

Ella Fitzgerald

I kept a diary right after I was born. Day 1: Tired from the move. Day 2: Everyone thinks I'm an idiot.

Steven Wright

You know you're getting old when you get that one candle on the cake. It's like, 'See if you can blow this out.'

Jerry Seinfeld

I wanted to buy a candle holder, but the store didn't have one. So I got a cake.

Mitch Hedberg

I think, at a child's birth, if a mother could ask a fairy godmother to endow it with the most useful gift, that gift should be curiosity.

Eleanor Roosevelt

I intend to live forever. So far, so good.

Steven Wright

It was on my fifth birthday that Papa put his hand on my shoulder and said, 'Remember, my son, if you ever need a helping hand, you'll find one at the end of your arm.'

Sam Levenson

I remember when the candle shop burned down. Everyone stood around singing 'Happy Birthday.'

Steven Wright

Love the giver more than the gift.

Brigham Young

Let them eat cake.

Marie Antoinette

Every day, every birthday candle I blow out, every penny I throw over my shoulder in a wishing well, every time my daughter says, 'Let's make a wish on a star,' there's one thing I wish for: wisdom.

Rene Russo

At her birthday, my seven-year-old daughter will say that she wants these big cakes and certain expensive toys as presents, and I can't say no to her. It would just break my heart. But when I was little, for birthdays we just played outside and we were happy if we got any cake.

Goran Ivanisevic

On every birthday, I ask my wife, 'What would you like this year?' and her instant reply is, 'Diamonds! Diamonds! Diamonds!' I'm always living in hope that one day she'll say she just wants me!

Akshay Kumar

To me - old age is always ten years older than I am.

Bernard Baruch

If I have the power to post 'Happy Birthday' on someone's Facebook page and make them feel really good, it feels really good to make other people feel really good. I love it. I'm a huge Facebook and Twitter person. And I love talking to my fans. It's fun.

Rebecca Mader

It is lovely, when I forget all birthdays, including my own, to find that somebody remembers me.

Ellen Glasgow

Youth has no age.

Pablo Picasso

I love the big fresh starts, the clean slates like birthdays and new years, but I also really like the idea that we can get up every morning and start over.

Kristin Armstrong

There are three hundred and sixty-four days when you might get un-birthday presents, and only one for birthday presents, you know.

Lewis Carroll

When I was young and it was someone's birthday, I didn't have the money to buy nice presents so I would take my mom's camera and make a movie parody for whoever's birthday it was. When I'd show it them, they'd die laughing. That reaction was a high for me, and I loved that feeling.

David Henrie

There is still no cure for the common birthday.

John Glenn

I'm not materialistic. I believe in presents from the heart, like a drawing that a child does.

Victoria Beckham

The main prank that we play with props is for people's birthdays. The special effects people will put a little explosive in the cake so it blows up in their face - that's always fun to play on a guest star, or one of the trainees or someone who's new.

Catherine Bell

It's odd the things that people remember. Parents will arrange a birthday party, certain it will stick in your mind forever. You'll have a nice time, then two years later you'll be like, 'There was a pony there? Really? And a clown with one leg?'

David Sedaris

Our birthdays are feathers in the broad wing of time.

Jean Paul

If every year is a marble, how many marbles do you have left? How many sunrises, how many opportunities to rise to the full stature of your being?

Joy Page

Every year on my birthday, I start a new playlist titled after my current age so I can keep track of my favorite songs of the year as a sort of musical diary because I am a teenage girl.

Chris Hardwick

I quit high school on my birthday. It was my senior year and I didn't see the point. This was 1962, and I was ready to make music.

Barry White

I do like to shock and surprise people. When it's all in good fun, of course.

Ruth Warrick

To give somebody your time is the biggest gift you can give.

Franka Potente

If I could be doing anything, I'd be laying on the floor in my birthday suit eating junk food and watching something dumb on TV.

Anita Baker

We'll take the cake with the red cherry on top.

Navjot Singh Sidhu

My policy on cake is pro having it and pro eating it.

Boris Johnson

A gift consists not in what is done or given, but in the intention of the giver or doer.

Lucius Annaeus Seneca

I get uncomfortable when people give me presents and watch me open them. I don't have birthday parties, because the idea of a group of people singing and looking at me while I'm blowing out candles gives me hives.

Brit Marling

We all have special numbers in our lives, and 4 is that for me. It's the day I was born. My mother's birthday, and a lot of my friends' birthdays, are on the fourth; April 4 is my wedding date.

Beyonce Knowles

At my age flowers scare me.

George Burns

The best way to remember your wife's birthday is to forget it once.

E. Joseph Cossman

My biggest hero, Gregory Peck, was my birthday present on April 14, 1973. I just sat and stared at him.

Loretta Lynn

Handmade presents are scary because they reveal that you have too much free time.

Douglas Coupland

My life is better with every year of living it.

Rachel Maddow

My happiest memory of childhood was my first birthday in reform school. This teacher took an interest in me. In fact, he gave me the first birthday presents I ever got: a box of Cracker Jacks and a can of ABC shoe polish.

Flip Wilson

For my birthday I got a humidifier and a de-humidifier... I put them in the same room and let them fight it out.

Steven Wright

Most of us can remember a time when a birthday - especially if it was one's own - brightened the world as if a second sun has risen.

Robert Staughton Lynd

I think there's something about the homemade birthday cake, because my wife, on my daughter's first birthday, started the tradition where she takes a full cake and cuts the number birthday out of it.

Willie Geist

If you can give your child only one gift, let it be enthusiasm.

Bruce Barton

I'm not going to be caught around here for any fool celebration. To hell with birthdays!

Norman Rockwell

People give one another things that can't be gift wrapped.

Nadine Gordimer

A friend never defends a husband who gets his wife an electric skillet for her birthday.

Erma Bombeck

When someone asks if you'd like cake or pie, why not say you want cake and pie?

Lisa Loeb

I like to give people novels I think they would like, on no particular occasion - just when we're in a bookstore together. I like to receive reference books on my birthday.

Daniel Handler

For me, the end of childhood came when the number of candles on my birthday cake no longer reflected my age, around 19 or 20. From then on, each candle came to represent an entire decade.

Yotam Ottolenghi

I was forced to live far beyond my years when just a child, now I have reversed the order and I intend to remain young indefinitely.

Mary Pickford

Only then, approaching my fortieth birthday, I made philosophy my life's work.

Karl Jaspers

When I was in elementary school, I used to write letters to myself. I'd write letters and go 'Dear Kristen-at-16-years-old, happy birthday. I hope you're doing something.'

Kristin Kreuk

The return of my birthday, if I remember it, fills me with thoughts which it seems to be the general care of humanity to escape.

Samuel Johnson

A gift, with a kind countenance, is a double present.

Thomas Fuller

Like many women my age, I am 28 years old.

Mary Schmich

I'm amazed. When I was 40, I thought I'd never make 50. And at 50 I thought the frosting on the cake would be 60. At 60, I was still going strong and enjoying everything.

Gloria Stuart

I like to go to anybody else's birthday, and if I'm invited I'm a good guest. But I never celebrate my birthdays. I really don't care.

Mikhail Baryshnikov

To my surprise, my 70s are nicer than my 60s and my 60s than my 50s, and I wouldn't wish my teens and 20s on my enemies.

Lionel Blue

My ace in the hole as a human being used to be my capacity for remembering birthdays. I worked at it. Whenever I made a new friend, I made a point of finding out his or her birthday early on, and I would record it in my Filofax calendar.

Susan Orlean

I have 'Happy Birthday' in multiple languages on my iPod - I like to play it at company birthday parties.

Yigal Azrouel

The worst part about celebrating another birthday is the shock that you're only as well as you are.

Anne Lamott

I binge when I'm happy. When everything is going really well, every day is like I'm at a birthday party.

Kirstie Alley

I had a birthday one night on a farm we were shooting on. I walked into the tent, and there were 150 people waiting for me, all wearing masks of my face.

Stephen Hopkins

The reason I met my husband was because I remembered a friend's birthday. The moral of the story is: Remember people's birthdays.

Julianna Margulies

When I was little I thought, isn't it nice that everybody celebrates on my birthday? Because it's July 4th.

Gloria Stuart

My mother asked me what I wanted for my birthday, so I said I wanted to read poetry with her.

Guy Johnson

I am a big popcorn fanatic. I love popcorn. In fact one year for my birthday, my husband bought me one of those big popcorn machines like they have in movie theaters.

Debbie Macomber

I jumped out of an airplane on my 34th birthday because I promised myself I would. I have an interest in confronting my fears.

Michael Trucco

I have an extensive library - every birthday when I was a kid my parents would ask what movie or book I wanted, so I have built up a big collection over the years.

Mark Bridges

Your children need your presence more than your presents.

Jesse Jackson

I cried on my 18th birthday. I thought 17 was such a nice age. You're young enough to get away with things, but you're old enough, too.

Liv Tyler

I'm a summer baby, so I usually have my birthday as a good summer memory.

Sloane Crosley

This is a wonderful way to celebrate an 80th birthday... I wanted to be 65 again, but they wouldn't let me - Homeland Security.

Art Buchwald

In 1993 my birthday present was a star on Hollywood's Walk of Fame.

Annette Funicello

For my birthday my husband learned to cook and is cooking one day a week for me. But he only likes to do fancy dishes. So we end up with weird, obscure things in the refrigerator.

Cheryl Hines

My mom FedExes a red velvet cake she makes from scratch to me every birthday.

Molly Sims

My mother still sends a cake to the office for my birthday.

David Ulevitch

As a child, I always chose a false nose and some face paint and a wig for my birthday.

Ashley Jensen

Most of us have fond memories of food from our childhood. Whether it was our mom's homemade lasagna or a memorable chocolate birthday cake, food has a way of transporting us back to the past.

Homaro Cantu

Any time women come together with a collective intention, it's a powerful thing. Whether it's sitting down making a quilt, in a kitchen preparing a meal, in a club reading the same book, or around the table playing cards, or planning a birthday party, when women come together with a collective intention, magic happens.

Phylicia Rashad

We invest less in our friendships and expect more of friends than any other relationship. We spend days working out where to book for a romantic dinner, weeks wondering how to celebrate a partner or parent's birthday, and seconds forgetting a friend's important anniversary.

Mariella Frostrup

The day which we fear as our last is but the birthday of eternity.

Lucius Annaeus Seneca

There is really a je ne sais quoi about turkey cooking - the air of festivity, the family squabbles, the constant basting - that does not apply to the turkey breast, which is, really, a convenience of food... A turkey without seasonal angst is like a baseball game without a national anthem, a winter without snow, a birthday party without candles.

Laurie Colwin

I joined the army on my seventeenth birthday, full of the romance of war after having read a lot of World War I British poetry and having seen a lot of post-World War II films. I thought the romantic presentations of war influenced my joining and my presentation of war to my younger siblings.

Walter Dean Myers

Success is like reaching an important birthday and finding you're exactly the same.

Audrey Hepburn

Since graduation, I have measured time in 4-by-5-inch pieces of paper, four days on the left and three on the right. Every social engagement, interview, reading, flight, doctor's appointment, birthday and dry-cleaning reminder has been handwritten between metal loops.

Sloane Crosley

The turning point was when I hit my 30th birthday. I thought, if really want to write, it's time to start. I picked up the book How to Write a Novel in 90 Days. The author said to just write three pages a day, and I figured, I can do this. I never got past Page 3 of that book.

James Rollins

I started running around my 30th birthday. I wanted to lose weight; I didn't anticipate the serenity. Being in motion, suddenly my body was busy and so my head could work out some issues I had swept under a carpet of wine and cheese. Good therapy, that's a good run.

Michael Weatherly

You always get a special kick on opening day, no matter how many you go through. You look forward to it like a birthday party when you're a kid. You think something wonderful is going to happen.

Joe DiMaggio

A diplomat is a man who always remembers a woman's birthday but never remembers her age.

Robert Frost

Yes, I am scared of prison. It's the last thing if you are after building up a business over 38 years and you are approaching your 66th birthday and you never owed a man a penny and you feel hard done by and you try to protect yourself and your family and go to prison - if that is the society we are living in, I am happy to accept that.

Sean Quinn

About astrology and palmistry: they are good because they make people vivid and full of possibilities. They are communism at its best. Everybody has a birthday and almost everybody has a palm.

Kurt Vonnegut

It was my 16th birthday - my mom and dad gave me my Goya classical guitar that day. I sat down, wrote this song, and I just knew that that was the only thing I could ever really do - write songs and sing them to people.

Stevie Nicks

Some people won't go the extra mile, and then on their birthday, when no one makes a fuss, they feel neglected and bitter.

Anne Lamott

I can sing 'Happy Birthday' to you in twelve different places, but one of them is going to make you feel a certain thing, maybe it's a vulnerability, maybe an innocence, maybe another way is sexy and soulful or bluesy whatever it is, but with singers, exploring keys, I think, is important.

Idina Menzel

You know, maybe I was just born in the wrong time, but I love all things romantic. Puffy understands that. For my last birthday, he covered my hotel room floor with rose petals and had flowers and candles all over the room.

Jennifer Lopez

John Candy knew he was going to die. He told me on his 40th birthday. He said, well, Maureen, I'm on borrowed time.

Maureen O'Hara

If we celebrate Martin Luther King Jr.'s birthday at a time of presidential inaugurals, this is thanks to Ronald Reagan who created the holiday, and not to the Democratic Congress of the Carter years, which rejected it.

David Horowitz

I guess I could say I'm an actor, which I am, but that sounds like I'm putting down being a movie star, which, let's face it, is what I've become to many people. For myself, I'm a guy who was very insecure from about age 14 until the day I hit my 30th birthday.

Dennis Quaid

I wanted to be the next Dana Carvey. This was my ultimate goal. If I ever cut into a birthday cake and made a wish, I would wish to be on 'Saturday Night Live.' If I threw a coin into a fountain, I would wish to be on 'Saturday Night Live.' If I saw a shooting star, I would wish to be on 'Saturday Night Live.'

Jimmy Fallon

I promised myself: Before your 18th birthday, you're going to be at Jean Paul Gaultier. And it worked. I was hired.

Nicolas Ghesquiere

My mom had me at 16 and took me every place she went. I remember going on peace marches. She tried to take me to Woodstock - it was pouring rain. It was on my birthday, and I was crying so much in the car they turned the car around and dumped me at my grandmother's house... I had a little attitude.

Debi Mazar

I have had fans make me the big picture collages of the photo books; I have had fans send me birthday cakes... sing to me on my voicemail. I have had fans flash me. I have had older fans give me their bras and underwear onstage.

Sean Combs

As he approached his 28th birthday in February 1840, Dickens knew himself to be famous, successful and tired. He needed a rest, and he made up his mind to keep the year free of the pressure of producing monthly installments of yet another long novel.

Claire Tomalin

I suddenly realized how much I loved her when we attended Alfred Hitchcock's 75th birthday party last August. There was something magical about that night, and it made me see how much she really meant to me.

Rod Taylor

Having a birthday cake squashed into your face by young kids? Delicious. I always don a Santa suit at Christmas. Remaining childish is a tremendous state of innocence.

John Lydon

I was born full grown in the middle of a hurricane and an earthquake on 10 September 1954, 12.52 P.M. When I found out that I had missed lunch, I gave such a shout that the Earth stopped and spun backwards two days. That's why I celebrate my birthday on 8 September.

Jon Scieszka

I thought it would be cool to Skype with fans on their birthday and spend, like, a half-hour with them. I did a couple of two-hour Skypes. I just hang out with them and play songs and stuff. At first they're kind of shy, but after a while they open up. I've had a lot of people tell me I'm doing something no one has ever done before.

Austin Mahone

You know, we'd just had a birthday, he was... you know, he still had a future out of him, and all I can is he was just one of the most beautiful people in the world... a very gifted man, and it's a loss to the world, not just for us.

Robin Gibb

I often go to bed in my birthday suit. But I like teddies and cute little undies that match. I like a sexy bra and panty set, or little shorts.

Queen Latifah

New Year's Day is every man's birthday.

Charles Lamb

In January 1962, when I was the author of one and a half unperformed plays, I attended a student production of 'The Birthday Party' at the Victoria Rooms in Bristol. Just before it began, I realised that Harold Pinter was sitting in front of me.

Tom Stoppard

When Oscar Niemeyer died on December 5, 2012, ten days before his 105th birthday, he was universally regarded as the very last of the twentieth century's major architectural masters, an astonishing survivor whose most famous accomplishment, Brasilia, was the climactic episode of utopian High Modern urbanism.

Martin Filler

Ask any teenage girl to describe her perfect bedroom, and you'll get answers like 'a room with a private phone line, a place to hang out with friends, and for it to be way-cool and funky.' Ask parents the same question, and 'a locked door that opens on their 21st birthday' might top the list!

Candice Olson

I wrapped my Christmas presents early this year, but I used the wrong paper. See, the paper I used said 'Happy Birthday' on it. I didn't want to waste it so I just wrote 'Jesus' on it.

Demetri Martin

With my wife I don't get no respect. I made a toast on her birthday to 'the best woman a man ever had.' The waiter joined me.

Rodney Dangerfield

I had the worst birthday party ever when I was a child because my parents hired a pony to give rides. And these ponies are never in good health. But this one dropped dead. It just wasn't much fun after that. One kid would sit on him and the rest of us would drag him around.

Rita Rudner

I'm most comfortable in my birthday suit.

Amanda Seyfried

I gave a funny speech at my wife's birthday party, and I'm thinking, 'Hey, I've still got it.'

Larry David

It is ironic that the one thing that all religions recognize as separating us from our creator, our very self-consciousness, is also the one thing that divides us from our fellow creatures. It was a bitter birthday present from evolution.

Annie Dillard

Anybody can have a birthday. It requires nothing. Murderers have birthdays. It's the opposite of anything that I believe in. And I don't like at work where you stop everything to sing 'Happy Birthday' to someone. I feel like that's for children.

Mindy Kaling

I tried to bake a cake for my mother's birthday - it took me four hours. It was terrible, and I cried for three days.

Rachael Ray

My best kiss was on stage. Kelly Rowland from Destiny's Child gave me a really nice soft kiss on my lips during a performance on my birthday. It was amazing.

Chris Brown

I was standing right behind Marilyn, completely invisible, when she sang 'Happy birthday, Mr. President.' And indeed, the corny thing happened: Her dress split for my benefit, and there was Marilyn, and yes, indeed, she didn't wear any underwear.

Mike Nichols

I believe that at least 70 percent of parenting goes to the mother. In our house, I'm the one who knows about all the school stuff, helps with the homework, organizes the play dates, and remembers the birthday parties.

Cindy Crawford

I've got some incredible fans actually - so loyal and they make me birthday cards and Christmas cards. I got this package of poems and artwork based around the songs. They've got this thing called 'Floetry' where they all have to put in artwork.

They've set up their own competitions and stuff which is kind of amazing.

Florence Welch

I am the guy dressing up in, you know, the caveman outfit for the kids' birthday parties.

Rob Lowe

My parents screened 'Willy Wonka & the Chocolate Factory' for my 6th birthday, and I became fascinated by the idea of living in a candy land with chocolate rivers and lollipop trees.

Dylan Lauren

I'm a Virgo and I'm more - I don't want to say 'negative' - but I'm the girl who thinks no one's coming to my birthday party, no one's buying my clothes, no one's reading my book, no one's watching my show - that's just how I think.

Rachel Zoe

That's the great thing about New Year's, you get to be a year older. For me, that wasn't such a joke, because my birthday was always around this time. When I was a kid, my father used to tell me that everybody was celebrating my birthday. That's what the trees are all about.

Alan King

I hate birthdays. I hate birthday parties. I hate them. I don't know what it is, anybody's only got to come wafting near me with a piece of cake with a candle on and I break out in hives.

Cat Deeley

Funny story: I was hanging out with Adam Shankman for Samantha Ronson's birthday, and Lance Bass was there. I don't really know Lance, but he comes over to me and goes, 'Hey, I just wanted to let you know I'm a fan of 'Pretty Little Liars' and I'm rooting for your character.' It was surreal! That's how 'PLL' has changed my life.

Ryan Guzman

If there's one thing I really want for my birthday, that is for the mining company not to mine my daddy's reserve.

Bindi Irwin

I have an ambivalent relationship with Margaret Thatcher. She came to power in May 1979 - a month before my 11th birthday. I was far too young to have developed a great deal of political awareness. I remember it, though - my mother excited at the dinner table because Britain had its first female prime minister.

Sara Sheridan

Jewellery's not a big thing for me. The only thing I wear is a gold cross on a chain that I got for my 21st birthday. You have to take it off every day for filming, but that's the only time I'm not wearing it. You won't find me in rings, bracelets or earrings.

Jonas Armstrong

Friends and family do not believe you write fiction. They truly believe that every word you write is either autobiographical or based on them. I once had a character say that she never wanted to be invited to another children's birthday party, and I never received another children's birthday party invitation ever again.

Liane Moriarty

When I auditioned for drama college, they asked me to do my Shakespeare. I couldn't do it. They asked me to do my modern, and I couldn't do it. They asked me if I had a song prepared, and I said 'No,' so I sang 'Happy Birthday.' And I did a reasonable improvisation, a reasonable one, nothing special at all. I don't know how I got in, but I did.

Hans Matheson

As I approached my 95th birthday, I was burdened to write a book that addressed the epidemic of 'easy believism.' There is a mindset today that if people believe in God and do good works, they are going to Heaven.

Billy Graham

I'm not a big birthday guy; I never have been.

Lewis Black

I just had my 30th birthday and we went turkey shooting. It's what I wanted to do, so we went.

Kelly Clarkson

I think the best thing about my job is that I have my life documented, which not many people get to have. They have a photo here and there and maybe some video footage from a birthday. My kids will be able to see me growing up.

Kirsten Dunst

I threw my 20th birthday party at Brown, and I didn't even have to say to anyone not to put pictures on Facebook. Not a single picture went up. That was when I knew I'd found a solid group of friends, and I felt like I belonged.

Emma Watson

The American flag is an enduring symbol of liberty, democracy, and justice. It is fitting that the House act to protect it as we approach our nation's birthday, and as our men and women in uniform rally behind it in Iraq's battlefields.

Joe Barton

I've always wanted to buy a sports car. After the England series, I went up to my dad and said that I wanted to buy a sports car and got his consent. On his birthday, I surprised him by bringing it home. It's a Porsche Boxter Limited Edition, and my family was thrilled to see it.

Suresh Raina

Interventions are really emotionally exhausting and I would never ever want to have one. In the same way, I would never want to have a surprise birthday party. That would be horrible.

Margaret Cho

I want a chainsaw very badly, because I think cutting down a tree would be unbelievably satisfying. I have asked for a chainsaw for my birthday, but I think I'll probably be given jewelry instead.

Susan Orlean

When I was a kid, for my birthday every year, my mother made me pasta bechamel, which is rigatoni with a white cream sauce.

Giada De Laurentiis

I had been offered a Hollywood contract before my 18th birthday. It gave me the spark I needed.

Gene Tierney

A true nature is a gloomy monolith, sort of like that old black rotary phone that I had to sing 'Happy Birthday' to Grandpa on. But novelists, damn us, still need true natures - so we can give them to our protagonists. And so readers can vaguely predict how they'll behave when we trap them in 'situations' that they can't IM their way out of.

Walter Kirn

I used to be good with kids, but as I get older, I'm grumpy and terrible with them. As for doing a gig at a 6-year old's birthday party, you couldn't pay me enough.

Johnny Vegas

For the youth, the indignation of most things will just surge as each birthday passes.

Chris Evans

I'm not a birthday person. Maybe because I don't like to build expectations around that one day. You never know how it'll turn out to be.

Ranbir Kapoor

When I was six, my best friend's parents bought him a piano. My mother noticed that every time I would go to his house, the first thing I would say to him was 'Levester' - His name was Levester - I said, 'Levester, can I go play your piano?' So, on my 7th birthday, my parents bought me a piano.

Herbie Hancock

For Tim Burton's birthday I gave him a rainbow beetle. He loved it!

Eva Green

I played rugby for years, and I had a rugby jacket that I lost when I was 14. Somehow, my brother found it in storage 15 years later, and he gave it back to me for my 30th birthday. That was amazing and probably one of the best gifts I've ever received.

Ryan Reynolds

The Queen of Crafts herself, Martha Stewart, and I have the same birthday. I prefer to think it's the glue-gun wielding, perfect-tart-producing Martha and not the copper pan-throwing, jail-going Martha. But I suppose if I am going to share a calendar square with some of Martha, I have to share it with all of Martha.

Sloane Crosley

I want to say that probably 24 hours after I told CBS that I was stepping down at my 65th birthday, I was already regretting it. And I regretted it every day since.

Walter Cronkite

I had arranged a birthday party for him and my children, who are all Aquarians. Instead, we got married. I ran out of excuses. It was just us and my children.

Diane von Furstenberg

I got my first tennis racket on my seventh birthday. And because we had a tennis court in our backyard, I played every day. By ten I was playing competitively.

Tullian Tchividjian

I've never looked forward to a birthday like I'm looking forward to my new daughter's birthday, because two days after that is when I can apply for reinstatement.

Pete Rose

I wanted Cathy and Irving to actually say 'I do' and be pronounced husband and wife on Feb. 5, which is my mom's birthday.

Cathy Guisewite

I saw Richard Linklater's film 'Slacker' for my twenty-first birthday. That was the moment when it all seemed possible. This guy gave me hope.

Kevin Smith

All I watch is the Food Network. I took a cheesemaking class a few weeks ago, and I told my family and friends to only get me kitchen stuff on my birthday. I'm into every kind of cookbook and anything by Anthony Bourdain. I'd love to own a restaurant if I could find the right chef.

Jesse McCartney

Citizens, thank you for all your birthday wishes. I am 88 years old today and still lucky to live in the greatest city in the world.

Ed Koch

I had Hallowe'en parties every year, as it was my birthday five days before. My parents would actually put prosthetic noses on, and my dad would wear a top-hat and tails, put on a fake curly moustache, and hold a pipe.

Bat for Lashes

Every year before a big competition, I get hurt doing stuff I should not be doing. One year it was my little brother's 12th birthday. We all played hide-and-seek late at night. I climbed up a 30-foot tree, thinking he'd never catch me. I tripped and fell on one of the branches and I hit my head.

Ryan Lochte

My first paying job might have been doing a play, actually. My mom paid me to dress up as a flounder at my sister's 'Little Mermaid' - themed birthday party when I was little.

Paul Dano

We were probably the last people in the country to get a VCR and we didn't have cable. There wasn't any admiration of glamour, no, 'I want to look like them or have that lifestyle', because everyone in my town had the same lifestyle. So I didn't think, 'Ooh, a movie star's birthday!' I just thought, 'What?'

Christina Hendricks

If Congress can move President's Day, Columbus Day and, alas, Martin Luther King's Birthday celebration for the convenience of shoppers, shouldn't they at least consider moving Election Day for the convenience of voters?

Andrew Young

I tend to foster drama via bleakness. If I want the reader to feel sympathy for a character, I cleave the character in half, on his birthday. And then it starts raining. And he's made of sugar.

George Saunders

The thrill of performing - that's something that hasn't changed for me. That simultaneous joy of creating something and sharing it with an audience - it's the same now as it was then, when it was just my cousins' birthday party.

Steve Buscemi

And for the city's birthday, we will host events in every neighborhood of the city, inviting all of our residents to share in the celebration of Boston's great epic - the story of neighbors who support one another where it matters most.

Thomas Menino

I married two weeks after my 18th birthday, far too young, and by the time I was 23 I was a single mother of three small children, Sean, Daniel and Victoria, living in a prefab house.

Sue Townsend

I timed my previous wife's pregnancy to the moment to have my son born on Bob Dylan's 50th birthday. There is no bigger Bob Dylan fan than me. You don't just time the day and impregnate your wife to get your kid to be born on Bob Dylan's 50th birthday.

Charlie Trotter

I can remember the three restaurant experiences of my childhood. All I wanted to do on my birthday was to go to the Automat in New York... but I don't know if you consider that a real restaurant.

Alice Waters

In the Mexican culture, we never miss a baptism, a birthday, a baby shower, a wedding shower, a wedding. You must show up. Otherwise, you'll be in big trouble.

Eva Longoria

Birthday Alarm was a very simple site based on being reminded of your friends' birthdays.

Michael Birch

I'm over the moon to be involved in the 'Doctor Who' Christmas special. I can't quite believe it as it's a part of the family tradition at the Jenkins household. I heard the news that I got the role on my 30th birthday and it was the best birthday present ever.

Katherine Jenkins

Why, on my mother's birthday, am I thinking about 'Father Knows Best?' At our house, mother knew best at least as often as father did, but then the title of the old sitcom, a homogenized portrait of American family life, was meant to be slightly sardonic.

Tom Shales

I crashed my boyfriend's birthday when I was 12 years old. He didn't invite me and so I showed up.

Isla Fisher

If you catch me lying, it's probably because I'm about to surprise someone for their birthday, or hide away the specific details about a company getaway to a strange but amazing place.

Ryan Holmes

As I approach my 88th birthday, it's become apparent to me that my eyes and ears, among other appurtenances, aren't quite what they used to be. The prospect of long flights to wherever in search of whatever are not quite as appealing.

Mike Wallace

My second play, The Birthday Party, I wrote in 1958 - or 1957. It was totally destroyed by the critics of the day, who called it an absolute load of rubbish.

Harold Pinter

Robert Duvall saw me playing at a restaurant in Louisiana and invited me to be an extra in his movie 'The Apostle.' He gave me a guitar for my sixth birthday, and I thought that was the coolest thing in the world.

Hunter Hayes

I worked at an ice cream parlor called Chadwicks. We wore old-timey outfits and had to bang a drum, play a kazoo, and sing 'Happy Birthday' to people while giving them free birthday sundaes. Lots of ice cream scooping and $1 tips.

Amy Poehler

I've been a Nick Cave fan since the early '80s when he was part of The Birthday Party thing singing Australian self-destructive rock band and I've always followed his work and loved it.

Aleksandar Hemon

The more Mommy blogs going nuclear over playground etiquette I read and birthday parties of glazed adults munching cupcakes like demoralized zombies I attend, I realize this is what my friends who conceived before me meant by, 'You just won't care.'

Emma McLaughlin

I've got more than 600 pairs of Ray-Ban sunglasses, from 1950s originals to newer models. I have them on the wall like opticians do so I can pick out a pair that goes with my outfit. I had around 30 pairs, then my husband Rainer started getting them for me as birthday and Christmas gifts.

Suzi Quatro

I know that might sound silly coming from someone my age, but I remember on my 14th birthday having a crisis like my mom should be having. I kept thinking that I was getting older, and I haven't really accomplished anything. I remember thinking that I better accomplish something real soon.

Q'orianka Kilcher

Well, I started conducting kind of by accident. I wanted to give myself a special birthday present for my fortieth birthday, and I was living in San Francisco at the time and I started attending some of the concerts and then simply dropping hints.

Bobby McFerrin

I've died so many times. I'm 65. On my 40th birthday, my girlfriend gave me a reel with ways I had died, whether it was by knife, or electrocution or drowning or being thrown off a building or whatever it might have been. I've died a lot of times!

Jonathan Banks

Brilliantly lit from stem to stern, she looked like a sagging birthday cake.

Walter Lord

I'm trying to get the record that I made at my birthday party last year, trying to get that out, and the lawyers are diddling around with it and it probably won't be out until next year. I don't know.

Marian McPartland

On a royal birthday every house must fly a flag, or the owner would be dragged to a police station and be fined twenty-five rubles.

Mary Antin

My birthday is a day when all I want is to bask in the love of my family and rarely accept offers for concerts and shows if they are to be held on this day.

Kailash Kher

We didn't have a whole lot of money when I was growing up either. I would always ask for magic books or magic tricks for my birthday or for Christmas and the rest of the year I either had to mow lawns or find part time jobs to help supplement the cost of doing magic.

Lance Burton

I turned 40 on the set of the reunion show for 'Sheer Genius,' so it wasn't a hideous birthday because I had everyone on the cast and crew sing 'Happy Birthday' to me, and I won $10,000 for being the fan favorite. It was really liberating to turn 40 and realize that I felt very comfortable with myself and knew who I was.

Tabatha Coffey

Every five years, I like to do a big birthday party. I had my 45th birthday with 75 friends in Marrakesh, Morocco.

Chip Conley

I love mayonnaise. Every birthday when I was a kid I'd go to Black Angus and just dip my burger in mayo.

Blake Anderson

Fourth of July. My birthday is July first, and my best friend's birthday is July fifth, so it's always been a favorite holiday. It's all about having a cooler full of sodas, hot dogs, and just hanging out and shooting off firecrackers, being low-key, watching the fireworks.

Hilarie Burton

I've looked after my money. As I started working around my third birthday, my first check went straight to the bank.

Samantha Barks

I was quite a shy child. I would get terribly nervous and throw up before my birthday party. And then I would be fine. I feel the same now. I get nervous, then it's fine.

Matthew Macfadyen

I went to a rare live Van Dyke show and met him there. And then he came to a show of mine and we spoke back stage. The third time was at Brian Wilson's birthday party.

Matthew Sweet

On my 14th birthday, my grandfather and my grandmother gave me the best birthday present ever: a drafting table that I have worked on ever since.

Jarrett J. Krosoczka

My son had his eighth birthday recently and we had a chance to borrow the film and show it to all of his friends that was at his birthday party and they loved it. I was a little nervous. I said they might not even like it, and say his daddy's movie is wack, but they loved it.

Blair Underwood

And currently, there are four to five new works in the pipeline for upcoming celebrations such as the Sydney 2000 Olympics, Australian Federation, my 50th Birthday, and Sydney Dance Company's 25th Anniversary.

Graeme Murphy

I wasn't very good about juggling family and my career. I was interested in who was coming to the children's birthday party, what my son was writing. I was thinking about Legos.

Jill Clayburgh

Motorcycle riding has been a passion of mine since my 20th birthday, and as a proud member of the American Motorcyclist Association and the Harley Owners Group, I can attest that responsible riding has many unique recreational benefits for millions of Americans.

Tim Walberg

I did a cake for the 60th birthday of Elton John, for Britney Spears' 27th birthday and for the 'Circus' album she put out - the cake had circus themes. I prepared a cake for a surprise 82nd birthday event for the architect Frank Gehry; the cake was comprised of mini-replicas of his buildings.

Ron Ben-Israel

If I have one wish for my birthday, it is that 35 is the end of desperation and the beginning of acceptance. Part of that is believing that if I'm meant to give birth, I will.

Jessi Klein

An army environment is very protected, a walled city kind of environment, where everybody has the same income, you have the same birthday parties, you are given return gifts - everything is the same. Everybody is moving up at the same pace.

Nimrat Kaur

I've raced on all seven continents at least twice. I've probably run thousands of races. But the single race that I'm most proud is a 10K. Yes, a 10K. I ran it with my daughter on her 10th birthday.

Dean Karnazes

I filed a brief as a friend of the court in the U. of Michigan to keep affirmative action at the U. of Michigan, which I attended the law school. And I was one of the original sponsors of making the Martin Luther King birthday a federal holiday.

Dick Gephardt

I lost twins at 14 weeks, and I had to have an D and C on my birthday.

Amy Weber

For my 23rd birthday, I received a nylon string guitar. I told myself that if I could play Eric Clapton's 'Tears In Heaven,' then I could play the guitar. I practised every chance I got, driving my housemates insane, until several weeks later I had a shaky version of the song down. I wrote my first song on the guitar a few weeks after that.

Neil Jackson

By the time of my ninth birthday, I had become a bit of a socialist, as I am said by conservative colleagues to be to this day. I went on within the next few years to volunteer as an envelope stuffer for the American Labor Party, and my political thinking has not shifted measurably since that time.

Sherwin B. Nuland

My parents were dishonest people. If it was my birthday, I knew my mother took me to the K-Mart and she stole my toy. She'd put it in the shopping cart and we'd walk out. I was raised with that.

Vincent Gallo

I have been a frequent air traveler since I was a few months shy of my sixth birthday, when my parents packed me off to boarding school two plane rides away from home. Those days of being willingly handed from air hostess to air hostess as an 'unaccompanied minor' made me blase about the rigors of air travel.

Shashi Tharoor

I hate birthdays. I thought that I only hated my own birthday, and then I realized that I hate my children's birthdays too.

Samantha Bee

Seven years into writing a novel, I started to lose my mind. My thirty-seventh birthday had just come and gone, the end of 2008 was approaching, and I was constantly aware of how little I had managed to accomplish.

Akhil Sharma

I saw Farrah Fawcett originally when she and her boyfriend, Lee Majors, came over to my house for a birthday party that I was having for my ex-wife, Leigh Taylor-Young.

Ryan O'Neal

I grew up doing all that stuff because I was obsessed with the '50s. I had sock hops for birthday parties. So I've always done The Twist and stuff. It was pretty natural and, with my parents doing it all the time, I'd just copy them. Not very pretty.

Brittany Snow

I got my first camera when I was 21 - my boyfriend gave it to me for my birthday - but at that point politics was my life, and I viewed the camera as a tool for expressing my political beliefs rather than as an art medium.

Carrie Mae Weems

I used to go down every year for the remembrance of Elvis' birthday. Memphis State College invited me to sit in the auditorium and speak to the people for one of those Elvis days.

Otis Blackwell

I'm really not the party type. I more like to have friends over at the house and chill. I've never been the super party type. But for the 18th birthday, you got to party. And then 21 is going to be even bigger.

Jacob Latimore

My 21st birthday was awesome. I was in L.A., and it was great. I had a bunch of friends that came out. The night ended up in a completely different direction than we thought it was going to go.

Jonathan Keltz

Even when I was a kid, I had a good thing with kids. To this day, if I go to a birthday party with one of my kids, I swear to you, I am so much happier hanging out with my kids and their friends than talking to the grown-ups.

Shawn Levy

And I was very shy as a kid; if you sang me 'Happy Birthday,' I would cry. Quite shy. So the idea of being an actor, much less a model, was just out of this world.

Cody Horn

I'm one of those people who had Christmas and my birthday always combined, and generally, my birthday was pretty much ignored. But my parents are always good about making some kind of special effort to make me feel like I also have a birthday that exists.

Noel Wells

My birthday is Feb. 11, and I'm both excited and not excited by it. You'll never be 15 again, and you really, really need to savor every day like it's your last.

Q'orianka Kilcher

I trained to be a priest - started to. I went to seminary school when I was 11. I wanted to be a priest, but when they told me I could never have sex, not even on my birthday, I changed my mind.

Johnny Vegas

It's in my stars to invent; I was born on Madame Curie's birthday. I have this need for originals, for innovation. That's why I like Charlie Parker.

Joni Mitchell

I celebrated my 18th birthday in Japan, which was quite memorable; I was quite fascinated by the different traditions and the culture; it was so completely different to Australian culture.

Miranda Kerr

I told my father I wanted to play the banjo, and so he saved the money and got ready to give me a banjo for my next birthday, and between that time and my birthday, I lost interest in the banjo and was playing guitar.

Jackson Browne

I'll never forget my 24th birthday when my tooth got punched out. And for a second I was like, it would be really hilarious if I sold it on eBay. But I can't, that's just too creepy. I don't think I can go there.

Evan Rachel Wood

My mom won't let me buy high-fashion stuff unless it's TK Maxx or a birthday occasion.

Chloe Grace Moretz

Mattresses! Beautiful! Let's go buy a couple of mattresses. Give 'em to people for their birthday.

Lawrence Tierney

I get letters constantly from all over the world, telephone calls from America, Brazil, Australia, all over, especially on my birthday. A family? I have a huge international family. That's all I need.

Renata Tebaldi

Nicole will come up in conversations where it's in a part of the conversation. Or we may be somewhere and I would tell some story about their mother and I. You know, we always honor her birthday.

O. J. Simpson

For my 50th birthday, I got ahold of a new print of 'Saturday Night Fever.' I see it much more as a tough coming-of-age movie than as a disco story.

Gene Siskel

I had sort of had a 21st birthday when I was 17, 18 years old living in Japan. I had all of that stuff sort of happen earlier for me, which happens to a lot of people. My 21st birthday was just a little boring. Not a great story.

Sarah Wright

One of the shocks of a 50th birthday is realizing the fundamental fact that your youth is irrevocably over.

Marianne Williamson

I saw a man killed in front of my eyes just before my eighth birthday.

Peter O'Toole

I left school on my 15th birthday.

David Bailey

I like working on my birthday, so I always do.

Abhishek Bachchan

If you are an actress in L.A., on your 40th birthday they should just hand you the keys to the lunatic asylum.

Romola Garai

All my favorite stars, my family and my friends are here. I'm having the happiest birthday that an 18-year-old girl could ever have.

Brandy Norwood

Washington's birthday is worthy of celebration - he is one of the greatest men in history. But Washington himself would likely have seen celebration of the office of the presidency itself as monarchic in nature.

Ben Shapiro

The day before my 16th birthday I got my guitar.

Stevie Nicks

The first guitar I ever got was for my 13th birthday.

Rick Springfield

I'm actually a perpetual 13-year-old. I've never advanced beyond 13. Every day, tomorrow is my 14th birthday. That's my kind of humor.

Terry Crews

As a kid, I always went to therapists; the first time was when my parents were separated on my sixth birthday, then on and off since then.

Pete Wentz

I can put my legs behind my head and sing 'Happy Birthday.' Because that's something that me and my friends used to do when we were in gymnastics class as kids, and I can still do it. I was doing it since I was 8 and 9. They used to call me Gumby. Very bendy.

Emmy Rossum

Growing up, my birthday was always Confederate Memorial Day. It helped to create this profound sense of awareness about the Civil War and the 100 years between the Civil War and the civil rights movement and my parents' then-illegal and interracial marriage.

Natasha Trethewey

My mom and my father's birthday are on the same day.

Victor Cruz

On my birthday, I was in Milan for the collections.

Eva Herzigova

I was fired at the pinnacle of my career, on my 39th birthday. And in the year that followed, I learned that there are many psychological phases of being 'let go.'

Mika Brzezinski

I have angel wings and a halo on my wrist, which I got done on my 30th birthday in memory of my brother.

Sheridan Smith

One I built when I was a kid, and it was a real miniature of Disneyland. I fell in love with the park when I went there with my parents on my 12th birthday.

Bobby Sherman

As far as those kinds of things, I also played at the concert to call for the release of Nelson Mandela when he was a political prisoner in South Africa. We were celebrating his 70th birthday and calling for his release.

Jackson Browne

There weren't any astronauts until I was about 10. Yuri Gagarin went into space right around my 10th birthday.

John L. Phillips

If I go away, I take a little picture of my son. It's in a frame with a speaker, and he recorded a birthday message for me when he was nine or 10. I can't listen to it without filling up.

Lesley Manville

My first recognition of age setting in was exactly on my 36th birthday. I have no idea why, on this day of all days, I looked in the mirror and realized my face no longer looked young.

Paulina Porizkova

I always wanted to shave. It is a very natural process. For my birthday I got a lot of shaving stuff.

Chaz Bono

I love having my birthday at Australia Zoo.

Bindi Irwin

I sing a little bit. I got a guitar for my 16th birthday.

Jesse Plemons

With my daughter, we do arts and crafts, we read a lot, we listen to music, and we cut the strings off balloons and bounce them around after birthday parties.

Lisa Loeb

I think I've wanted to be an actress since the day I was born. I even asked my parents for an agent for my seventh birthday!

Shoshannah Stern

I'm an avid shoe fan. I got my first pair of Louboutins as a birthday gift from Jami Gertz.

Toks Olagundoye

When you're an expert in a subject, you can retain new factoids on your favorite topic easily. This only works for the subjects you're truly passionate about, though. Baseball fans can reel off stats for their favorite players, then space out on their own birthday.

Clive Thompson

My brother got a .22 for his 12th birthday; I got a .22. He got a hunting knife; I got a hunting knife.

Stephanie Cutter

I have friends who hide in their bedroom for three days every time they have another birthday. That's what brings the wrinkles! I didn't care when I turned 30 or 40 or 50.

Maria Conchita Alonso

I was fired by 'America's Next Top Model' on my birthday.

Paulina Porizkova

I love photography. My boyfriend's got a great camera, which I bought for his birthday.

Sarah Sutton

My husband, Bill, and I tried having kids naturally, but then I came to a crossroads before my 40th birthday: I realized that my being a mother wasn't limited to my bearing a child. I just knew that I wanted to be a mother, so I offered it up to my destiny to God and to the universe and met with an adoption attorney. The process was not difficult.

Christine Ebersole

One thing that was really dope for me was that my dad had a '78 Corvette, '78 or '76 Corvette all my life. It always needed to be fixed up. I remember it's just been sitting in the driveway for years, and I got it fixed from top to bottom for his birthday.

Sevyn Streeter

When I was 11, I had an Ugly Sister birthday party. All my idea. Most girls want to be a fairy or a princess, but there I am with beauty spots and fur and fluorescent pink kiss-curls.

Lucy Punch

I dated a guy for over a year who lied about his age the entire time. I found out after the fact and couldn't believe it! I even threw him a birthday party for the wrong age... I couldn't get over how hard he had tried to keep it a secret!

Kirsten Prout

On my 30th birthday, all the presents I got were boxes of food. That's what I needed.

Kay Lenz

With a recent birthday, I've been acting now for twenty years.

Thayer David

If you've been running a business for 38 years, you're approaching your 66th birthday, you've never owed a man a penny or done anyone any grievance in your life, and you feel hard done-by and try to protect yourself and your family, but go to prison, well if that's the society we're living in, I'm happy to accept that.

Sean Quinn

The first comic book I ever read was an issue of 'Legion of Super-Heroes' where the earth was surrounded by all of these chains. I remember the cover; I got it at a birthday party.

Jonathan Hickman

Lucy took care of me on the set, and made sure that none of the crew cussed around me. She also had birthday parties for me and made sure that they were well attended.

Keith Thibodeaux

I never got a chocolate birthday cake; I got a carob one. And when I went to other kids' houses, I was very covetous of things like Cheez Whiz that I'd find in their refrigerators.

Amanda Marshall

I was very aware of Jeff Buckley. My brother actually bought me The Mamas And The Papas and Jeff Buckley for my birthday when I was in my early teens.

Imogen Poots

I always knew that good stuff would come along when I was older. So when I was 18, I longed to be 30; when I was 30, I longed to be 50. I've always looked forward to my next birthday.

Joanna Lumley

I play PC and Xbox games at home, and I just got a PSP as a birthday present.

Uwe Boll

I often imagine what it would be like if my father were still here to mark his 100th birthday, if Alzheimer's hadn't clawed away years, possibilities, hopes. What would he think of all the commemorations and celebrations?

Patti Davis

I'd be happy to live till 80 as long as I was comfortable and in good health. Mind you, ask me again on the eve of my 80th birthday. Even so, I hope we don't all start living to be 120. I'm not sure I'd cope with another 60 years.

Bonnie Tyler

The summer of 2002 at the Wilson birthday party I met Van Dyke again and I made plans to have dinner with him.

Matthew Sweet

Family time was very difficult when my girls were little, but I never missed a birthday; I was there for every major event.

Jeff Dunham

My dad bought me a dartboard for my 11th birthday, and I became intrigued by the game.

Eric Bristow

The summer before my third year of law school, I worked at a law firm in Washington, D.C. I turned 25 that July, and on my birthday, my father happened to be playing in a local jazz club called Pigfoot and invited me to join him. I hadn't spent a birthday with him since I was 3, but I agreed.

Deval Patrick

I used to go to musicals every birthday - that was my birthday present. We'd go to London, me and my two brothers and mum and dad. I think I saw 'Mamma Mia' about five times.

Lily James